YOUR DOT LIFE

www.finddotlife.com
finddotlife@gmail.com
12490 Hamilton Rd
Chattahoochee Hills, GA 30268

ISBN: 979-8-9888482-0-2 (paperback)

ISBN: 979-8-9888482-1-9 (ebook)

ISBN: 979-8-9888482-2-6 (hardcover)

ISBN: 979-8-9888482-3-3 (audiobook)

Ordering Information:

Special discounts are available on quantity purchases by corporations, associations, and others. For details, contact finddotlife@gmail.com or visit www.finddotlife.com.

YOUR DOT LIFE

POSITIVE METHODS TO REDUCE ANXIETY, STRESS, AND CLUTTER TO FIND YOUR LIFE'S FOCUS

R COREY WINFREY

CONTENTS

INTRODUCTION
MEET YOUR DOT LIFE HERE

"Perfection is not when there is no more to add, but rather, when there is no more to take away."
- Antoine de Saint-Exupéry

The goal of this book is to help you to understand what it means to live the Dot Life you deserve. So, let us begin there:

WHAT IS THE DOT LIFE?

The concept of Dot Life living is the evolution toward living your life with a complete focus on being involved with and engaging solely in activities that are enormously important to you—activities that are positive and stimulating. The comprehensive approach to Dot Life encourages intense focus on everything you do. The Who, What, When, Where, and How of Dot Life is present in every category of life, which we'll cover in detail throughout this book and series.

My own Dot Life journey has taught me to examine my existence and purpose here on Earth. My personal study of people of every socioeconomic status forced me to dig further into the goals I set for myself. As I looked closely at the lives of people I know, as well as people I observe in the media, I removed income goals as the top priority in my own life to focus instead on my available time. My decision to focus on what I do with my time brought me to the realization that my earlier money goals were insignificant and far exceeded what I need for who I am and what I enjoy.

Once you realize how limited your mind can become by *not* living a Dot Life, you will understand even more clearly what you need to live this lifestyle. Sitting still while having a morning cup of coffee never felt so rewarding for me as it does now. Completing a morning of purposeful thought and reflection on goals brings on a new excitement every day.

The Dot Life journey is one that will transform and open your mind to understanding what is truly important to you and how to live and share those things with others around you. This journey will provide a path to a life that constantly reminds you to live in focus and balance.

Your Dot Life starts with establishing your unique "dot"—a compilation of the things important to you in all areas of your life. Your dot is formed by completing the positive life actions listed below.

THE FOUR STEPS TO ACHIEVING DOT LIFE

1. Cleanse
2. Minimize
3. Grow
4. Share

What will you Cleanse? —People, Habits, Actions, Thoughts ("PHAT"): if any of these are negative around you, they need to be taken away.

What will you Minimize? —Reduce everything left after cleansing to the essentials: the things that are needed and important. This will shape your dot into the life you want to build on.

Where do you need to Grow? —Grow your dot with positive and productive activities. Add people to your life who will fuel and support the continuation of your Dot Life journey.

What should you Share? —When you have achieved a positive life, the easy part is to begin sharing the Dot Life with those around you. You will experience the joy that comes with watching your loved ones improve in their own lives. Your life agenda will become positive and will influence those around you. Welcome to your Dot Life.

A PORTRAIT OF YOU

Have you ever seen Vincent van Gogh's 1887 *Self-Portrait*[1], the one hanging in the Art Institute of Chicago? It is a magnificent painting and one of his most famous. What I find particularly interesting about it is that a huge portion of the painting is made not of brush strokes, but of little dots of paint. Walk up close to it—as close as museum security will allow anyway—and you can make out the individual dots. But take a step back and what emerges is a full portrait of the person. It is a perfect metaphor for the Dot Life.

Think of your life as a collection of dots. Living a Dot Life is when you intentionally zero in on one of those dots—that is, an aspect of your life—and focus on it to make it the way you want it to be. Focus on enough dots in your life and eventually you will step back to see the self-portrait you want to see.

The collection of dots within your self-portrait as you come in for a close look reveals the many facets of yourself that can be improved. Your finances are a dot. Your relationships are a dot. Your thoughts about yourself are a dot. And so on.

Your portrait, viewed by yourself and others from afar, gives the overall appearance of the well-put-together masterpiece that you want people to see. This is where most of us settle while struggling inside with the many negative factors that have us living empty and unfulfilled lives (we will discuss those further, later). What needs to be examined is the makeup of dots that form who you are.

I once noticed that when someone got close to me and was able to see my dots up close, I began to have a different mindset as my behavior toward the person changed; I became more standoffish and combative. I had to realize that I was not the person I wanted others—or even myself—to see up close. Once I took a closer look at who I was, I realized how much more I could improve, and I completely stopped critiquing and blaming others for the missteps I have experienced in my life.

Understanding that we all have flaws and issues regardless of where we stand financially or socially helped me to understand how we look at things. Most people focus on highlighting the best of themselves—by any means necessary—and covering up anything that shows a sign of failure or "less than," so I have learned to look at the portrait of life completely differently. No longer do status, things, or social media presence stand out for me in the picture that is presented; those things are now the smaller dots when I look at the picture. Similarly, there are dots that detail failure, heartache, pain, jealousy, and other perceived negativity that are overlooked or hidden in a canvas. To live a Dot Life is to remove those negative dots and replace them with positive ones.

Your picture is *your* picture and only you can reshape it into the positive and focused Dot Life it needs to be.

A DOT LIFE FOCUS OPENS YOU TO SUCCESS

The more I indulged in my Dot Life, the less significant "things" became to me. The reality of waking up in the morning with options became my priority. Moving to a rural environment after living in the city all my life provided me with a view of the world from a unique perspective. Not only did that sharpen my focus as to what I wanted to succeed at, but it also taught me better ways to appreciate and enjoy my success with life experiences ranging from daily walks to opening to cultural differences around the world. Ironically, focusing on my Dot Life allowed me to pay more attention to everything around me: people, the landscape, animals, weather patterns, and more. The world has opened for me as a huge palette of exploration. No longer do I allow media and social norms to control my narrative and interest.

YOUR DOT LIFE QUESTIONS

Your Dot Life questions ask:

- *WHO are you trying to impress?*
- *WHAT do you enjoy in life?*
- *WHEN are you available for the things you enjoy?*
- *WHERE do you find peace and happiness?*
- *HOW do you achieve the goals/ objectives you set for yourself?*

For example, in establishing your understanding of who you are trying to impress, Dot Life requires you to investigate your intentions behind everything you do: buying that car, clothes, house, or anything else you want others to see. Do the things you obtain satisfy you? Once I understood the true intention of consumerism—and that it is really about who we aim to please—I found it a little depressing.

Your Dot Life journey will present you with tough decisions when making purchases. Often, your mind convinces you that you deserve the things you can obtain

—even though the need for them is not there. I will give you an example. My closets were full of clothing items that I felt justified in purchasing for their range of color, the type of event they were for, their style, the season they were for, the fabric, etc. Did you notice I said "closets" plural? There was a time when I needed multiple closets to house the ridiculous number of items I possessed. I also observed friends and family around me changing out seasonal clothing and needing more space to accommodate additional purchases.

My decision that I needed to do something about this excess came after a single purchase of a shirt that I brought home, only to discover that I had already purchased the exact shirt!

A good example of the clothing purchases I made in the past vs. my choices for what I wear today are designer shirts vs. standard quality tee shirts. A typical designer shirt cost me $100–$250, and based on its cost, I would not wear it regularly. Because of its "exclusivity" the shirt would not often be seen by others. Ironically, I realized that the people I interact with—the ones I deem important in my life—could not care less about what I wear.

Still, when it came to those expensive purchases, I found them hard to part with, even though I barely wore them. Yet I made the gut-wrenching decision to remove all of them—the 20+ suits, the 60+ shirts, 20 to 30 pairs of shoes, 20+ pairs of jeans, 8 watches, multiple hats, and 10+ coats!

Once I removed everything, I experienced a feeling that was a total breath of fresh air for me. I had not realized that having less of something could bring me so much clarity in my life.

And my current preference to wear quality tee shirts that blend with any wardrobe style provides me with comfort and the confidence to focus less on what I am wearing—at far less cost than the previous designer options.

Once you establish that WHO you aim to please is genuinely you and your Dot Life is in order, you will begin to see everyone and everything around you differently. Your Dot Life will become your mentality as you question each decision. Do I need this? Will I use it regularly? Does it add value to the things I have a passion for? Does the purchase make me happy, or does it simply make me feel included?

Dot Life protects you mentally, physically, financially, and spiritually from the things that get in the way of what you want in life. Time? Knowledge? Finances? To get to the point of understanding what you genuinely enjoy, you must remove the distractions, obstacles, and negative therapies that provide temporary Band-Aids and never get you to your true enjoyment.

Living a Dot Life means intentionally zeroing in on each of the dots that is an aspect of your life and focusing on it to make it the way you want it to be. Focus on enough dots in your life and, eventually, you will step back to see the self-portrait you want to see.

At some point, I realized that I had been working on the many dots of my makeup for years prior to my approaching the process intentionally. I had begun reducing my chaos in all areas, starting at various times in my life. Once I realized the peace it brought me, I began to apply that effort intentionally, which began an obsession to be free of anything that does not promote a healthy and happy dot.

To be intentional eventually became a way of thinking and a part of my conscious mindset in all areas of my life.

CHAPTER ONE

MY DOT STORY

HOW IT ALL BEGAN

My Dot Life journey started unintentionally in my thirties with the beginning stages of thinning hair.

As a young man in my early thirties, life was beginning to flourish. Income flowing, travel around the world increasing, having a wardrobe befitting a successful businessperson, cars, jewelry—the whole nine was coming together nicely. This stage of my life was the one where everything we work for is put on display for the world to notice. With that comes the task of being well groomed from head to toe. The chaos of managing life had not yet set in for me as it was all still new and exciting. Having the resources to manage whatever came my way without giving it a thought allowed me to feel invincible at the time. Imagine being in full control of everything you want to do and achieve. There was no limit or obstacle that could alter any decision I wanted to make in my life.

However, one day, sitting in the barber's chair, all of that changed. I recalled my barber telling me something I did not want to hear: "Rich—Your usual hairstyle is not going to work this time. As the expert behind your haircuts, I must let you know that your hair is not growing as thick as it used to. But of course, you were already aware of that."

Now, the last thing a man wants to hear from his barber is that his hair is thinning. I cannot imagine a man —or woman—reading this book, who can say that such a call out from your hair stylist would not bother you. Hair is supposed to be that beautiful masterpiece that crowns the whole ensemble of you—especially when you are conscious of your image. Your hair makes you look younger and more attractive!

While my sadness about the barber's announcement —a fact I had been ignoring—was not due to vanity, I must admit I knew I would miss the days of not having to think about my hair. In other words, hair had become my new worry. Now, I had to start considering my options.

Many readers know about the "Wild Wild West" of the hair replacement business in the marketplace today. There are hair-loss replacement systems, spray-on solutions, and the wearing of hats—all of which are effective ways to mask balding. However, each option gave me pause.

Were any of these solutions options I wanted to embrace? Instead of diving into the various methods for correcting the inevitable balding to come, I decided to observe my surroundings and consider how I felt about the results that others with the same issue had experienced. As I observed, I realized increasingly that I had no interest in partaking in any of the ceremony that others engage in to maintain their former glory. A new thing was happening to me. Why not roll with it?

I decided to shave off all my hair and live my life as a clean-shaven individual from that point.

That decision allowed me to avoid the numerous tactics to hide my balding and led to the simple task of shaving my head at home and avoiding the painful weekly visit to my barber. I dreaded having to engage in barber-shop "shop talk" that I considered male gossip or non-innovative discussion and I realized later that my decision to embrace my hair loss and eliminate my hair completely allowed me to dispense with shop talk altogether.

This was the birth of the idea in my mind. The idea of life simplification.

Each of the hair-loss solution options would have required some kind of continuous effort and, in fact, a financial commitment. I would have to cough up the funds for the hair replacement surgery. Or I would have to keep my bathroom cabinet stocked with spray-on hair. Or, I would have to store up hats in my wardrobe and always wear one out, even in the middle of sweltering summer heat.

Every one of those options was a task. It was a complication in my life. It would add expense to my financial balance sheet, and it would cause me grief because I would always have to consider my hair solution for the day.

Thus, why not keep it simple? Why not shave off the hair completely and get rid of the problem of what to do about my hair daily? I would have no hair to think about when I got up in the morning or when I needed to go out on the town. My "look" was a ready and clean-shaven one, and may I say that such a solution was exceptionally simple, and it made my life remarkably easy?

In case the point has not sunk in yet, let me expound on how simple my hair routine has now become: I can start my day's grooming routine by getting out of bed, strolling to the bathroom, brushing my teeth, taking a shower—and as I stand in front of the mirror to adjust my neck tie or slap on some cologne, I do not have a care in the world when it comes to hair grooming.

I do not need a hairbrush.

I may or may not decide to apply pomade to my shaved head.

I do not need to decide on the fashionable hat of the day that I want to wear to cover a balding pate.

I do not have to worry about whether sweat, humidity, or rain conditions during the day will interfere with a spray-on solution and cause my vainly sprayed-on hair to come sweltering down over my forehead in an embarrassing melt.

I start my day in front of the mirror without a thought about hair.

I end my day in front of the mirror without a thought about hair.

It is the perfect end-to-end worry-free hair life; a perfect circle that begins with no chaos and ends with no chaos!

Why had I not thought of this before? Why did I

never ponder the solution that a life can be built around a perfect circle of routines? Start the day with a worry-free routine and you will end the day in the same way! It was a circle. A perfect picture.

If I drew up my day of no hair worries, it would begin at Point A where I do not need a hairbrush, spray-on hair, or a hat—and it would end at Point Z where I do not need a hairbrush, spray-on hair, or a hat.

A perfect circle.

That is where the Dot Life was born for me. I began to incorporate the concept into every other area in my life. I felt compelled to investigate minimizing everything about my life to continue to feel free with fewer complications and less stress.

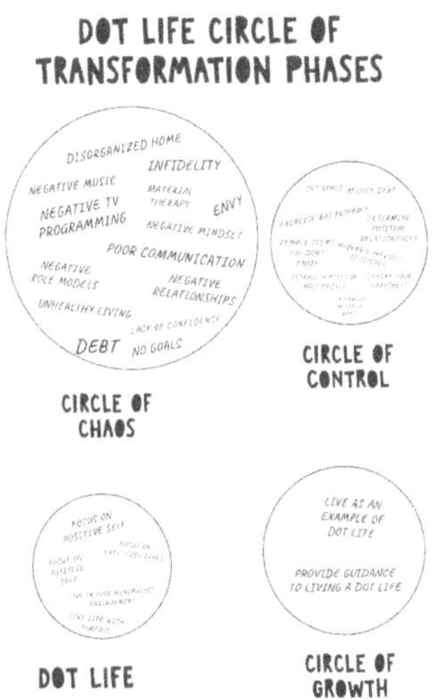

MAKING A CIRCLE

My journey had begun. My "circle" chronicles a life that can manifest because it is so simplified.

What does your circle look like? It could include so much that a focus is impossible to manifest.

My focus to Dot Life in this scenario is clear. I decreased my grooming routine and all that came with it to its most minimal state.

As I began to study every aspect of my life and the lives of everyone around me and beyond, I noticed that happiness was not a result of the things I had been led to believe it was. I had always believed that happiness was a "comfortable" place. To continue to strive for happiness based on what is comfortable to me and my current surroundings only made it easier for me to become distracted from pursuing things that truly made me happy. "Comfortable" is not necessarily happiness; it can be a distraction that keeps you in a place of unhappiness.

After experiencing the financial collapse of 2008[1] and the coronavirus pandemic of 2020, I am focused more than ever on living a Dot Life. The events that occurred during both events gave me a clear understanding of the importance of protecting my dot at all costs. I began to expand my understanding of the Dot Lifestyle.

During these events in my life, I learned that immersing myself in the Dot Life allowed me to be best prepared for downturns and unexpected negative events. During the 2008 real estate crash, I was not prepared to withstand the crisis—as most of us were not. I did not have my dot in order, which would have provided me a more creative space to maneuver through it better than I did. During the 2020 pandemic I was strategically prepared to withstand the financial standstill we all faced.

With my dot more focused on specific projects and project goals, my overall objectives were minimal: simply to focus on and to get through the unfortunate crisis.

The Dot Life journey, at key milestones, will provide you with a feeling of clarity and will motivate you to continue to strive for success.

In this book, I will take you on the same journey that I embarked on in understanding my perfect Dot Life. I will attempt to provide insight into each one of these milestones of achieving a Dot Life:

Circle Of Life
    Circle of Chaos / Bad Habits
    Cause of Chaos
    Cause of Bad Habits

Circle of Control
    Setting Goals
    Reduce Chaos / Bad Habits

Dot Life
    Minimalist Life System
    Creating New Self-focus

Eliminating all Negative / Non-Productive Influences

Circle Rebirth
Focus on Learning / Creating
Live Your Positive System
Share and Grow Your System

CHAPTER TWO

CIRCLE OF LIFE
THINKING ABOUT ORDER

Have you ever heard of Chaos Theory[1]? It is a concept that is usually applied to the mathematics field; however, other disciplines have adopted it over the years. In sociology and other social sciences, for example, the theory represents "complicated systems of order." It speaks to a society that is made up of systems that by nature are complicated.

This is exactly how the average human being lives. Our societies are supposed to be made up of systems—such as for working, commuting, shopping, etc.—that make life easier for us. These are supposed to be "ordered" systems. True, they may have many facets and prongs and features in them, but at the end of the day, they should make life easier for the average person.

Let us consider an example: When you want to order takeout for dinner, it is probably because you do not have the time to cook up something for yourself or your family that night. Society has developed several options wherein the typical family can "simplify" their life and order takeout.

Would you care to choose Uber Eats to deliver your food? Or DoorDash?

Wait a second—you should consider cooking something fresh for your family after all and order a meal kit like Chefs Plate. It is still technically a takeout—all the ingredients are already premeasured and prepackaged. You just need to toss it on the stove or in the oven and you have a home-cooked meal ready.

Oh dear. But there is HelloFresh, too. You have heard from several friends that HelloFresh is the absolute best when it comes to fresh vegetarian "home-made" food. You should go with HelloFresh for tonight.

Your system of dinner takeout is so simple: You do not want to do any heavy lifting for dinner tonight, and society has created an avenue for you to do that. Yet the system is so complicated too! You have just reviewed four different options of takeout or home-made meals, and you have not come to a decision about what you are going to do for dinner!

How did a simple decision get so complicated?

This example represents every prong of the average person's life in our current society. Our systems, intended to make life easier, have complicated them.

We live in a world where bad habits can be easily bred, and life can doubtless become a circle of chaos: You start out with a question of what to do for dinner, and you come full circle to the question of four dinner options to choose from, possibly more—and no decision.

Most individuals dwell in this chaos. It is not

surprising that you may find families who, every night, face the same dilemma of what to do for dinner. The decision-making process gets complicated as they consider the subject. They review their many options and they cannot agree on the right one that will work for everyone. The confusion comes full circle.

It repeats again. And again. And again.

I am guilty of the above. I am guilty of complicating things. I cannot imagine anyone in our current society who would say they are not. Though your vice may not be food ordering and how complicated it has made your life, it may be something else.

We live in a world that does not practice the "circle of life." You may not have heard of this term before.

The circle of life is, just as the phrase describes it, a circle. It starts at Point A, and it takes the individual back to Point A. For instance, let us use our food-ordering example. If you wanted to order takeout for tonight, and you are a believer in the circle of life, this is how your ordering process would look like:

You would have pre-considered the list of food-ordering options available to you: Chefs Plate, Uber Eats, DoorDash, and so on.

You would have analyzed which option suits your needs the most: Is the DoorDash phone app easier to use than Uber Eats? Are there better reviews of Chefs Plate than HelloFresh? Out of all these options, which one of them would provide you with a good, simple experience wherein you get the service you need, and you are not second-guessing yourself about whether it was the best option for you?

These thoughts are your pre-considerations. You will arrive at an answer. Without being partial to any service, let us say that you decide to choose DoorDash after your analysis.

You have noted that DoorDash has some helpful reviews. Their pricing is not as good as the others, or it may be better, but perhaps the phone-app experience overshadows the cost for you.

You choose DoorDash out of all the other options. You make your food order. And from that day forward, since your analysis has been done on the simplest, best option that works best for you, you continue to use DoorDash for your food-ordering needs. No complications regarding who to choose today.

No concerns about, "Do I need to download a new app by another provider?"

All these worries are gone because you have simplified your life regarding food ordering. You have achieved a perfect circle of life for that experience.

It is remarkably like the hair decision that I made and discussed earlier: decision made; life simplified. This is the circle of life.

I want to take you a step further into this life of ease. To go forward, we will have to talk about the obvious sad things that hinder us from achieving the perfect circle I have just described. In the next chapter, chaotic habits are identified as one of these vices that we all have.

CHAPTER THREE
CHAOTIC BAD HABITS
GETTING A HANDLE ON THEM

My unhealthy habits tend to creep up when things do not go as planned and I feel the need to have a crutch to get through failure or disappointment. When I retreat to those bad ways, I remind myself of the results that come from those behaviors. Repeating past unhealthy habits and mistakes became a focus of understanding that allowed me to concentrate on ridding myself of the bad behavior / habit before it altered my positive thinking or action. Bad behaviors for me provided a perceived comfort zone that I realized was a Band-Aid for stress, fear, and uncertainty. Unhealthy habits only prolong actions until you are forced to face them again. They do not go away, yet we are convinced that they will if we succumb to the vices.

There is probably no one who would suggest that they have never had bad habits. A bad habit denotes something that is out of control. They are the actions or inactions that people engage in that could be detrimental to their mental, physical, or financial health and negatively impact their well-being in other areas of their life as well.

A bad habit can come in many forms. Financially, it could be the habit of spending the credit card to its limit. Physically, it could be in the form of eating foods that you know are harmful to your health. Mentally, it could be as bad as engaging continually in relationships that are abusive and that harm the mental well-being of the abused individual—yet they keep getting involved in the same pattern of relationship. There is a lack of control in their decision-making and partner choices.

Earlier, in the My Dot Story chapter of this book, I provided some insight into the Dot Life: A perfect-circle life that begins with no chaos and ends with no chaos.

Reading this book, you may be outside that circle. At the moment, your life may be chaotic and chaos may reign in various areas of your life. In this section of the book, I am going to break down some areas in life that fuel the bad habits that keep us in chaos and away from the perfect Dot Life.

It is no news to anyone that habits can turn out to be extremely hard to break. The reason for this might vary from person to person, but the thing that bad habits have in common— whether it's the new diet that we have failed to complete or the work we procrastinate on until the very deadline—is that we can't seem to get rid of them no matter what we do.

Our unhealthy habits always find a way back to us. One of the main reasons we engage in them in the first place is stress, and it can be hard for us to resist things such as cigarettes and refined sugars. There are many other things—like wanting to take the easy route or being afraid of change—that can contribute to our unhealthy habits as well.

THE SCIENCE BEHIND BAD HABITS

The most important part of a human's body is the brain. Your brain is constantly generating stimuli that make you want to consume or make you crave things that might be bad for your health. There are three parts to this:

1. There is a trigger involved, e.g., stress.
2. Then there is a behavior in which you act, e.g., binge eating unhealthy food.
3. Last, there is a reward that makes you feel happy and satisfied.

The reason we do certain things this way is because of the good feeling we get instantly. These kinds of endeavors *do* give us instant satisfaction, but they might not be ideal for our health. In time, these become your automatic responses to certain things in life, which is why they turn into your daily habits.

You might hear "just try leaving it," from a lot of people, but the truth is, letting go of unhealthy habits is easier said than done. Our brains may seem like they are hard-wired, but we can mend these wires. We have the potential to rewire our brains in a way that helps us in adapting to all kinds of changes and helps to promote good and positive behaviors.

THE CAUSE OF BAD HABITS

The simplest way of seeing how a habit incorporates itself into your daily life is by seeing how you get triggered to brush your teeth before going to bed. Your act of brushing your teeth is a part of your routine, and the reward is the feeling of freshness in your mouth and good check-ups with your dentist.

Similarly, your negative behaviors also offer you some perceived great rewards. These bad habits are examples of outlets that people turn to that provide instant relief mentally at the moment but do nothing to resolve the issue that will continue to inflict damage and pain long term. The difference is that the reward is instant, which gives you satisfaction. It could be drinking in the club after a day of stressful work or smoking a cigarette when encountering a stressful situation.

CAUSE OF CHAOS

The literal meaning of the word "chaos" is complete confusion and disorder. This meaning of chaos is distinct from its scientific meaning, which refers to a phenomenon that is unpredictable. Chaotic behavior appears in individuals' lives for a variety of complex reasons. Chaos for me was camouflaged in my desire to appear well-rounded in all the areas of my life that I thought appealed to the people I associated with. I was acquiring things, attending events, and living a lifestyle that did not allow me time to focus on me and my core happiness and interests. When you realize that you are constantly thinking, "I hate having to do this," or "I don't enjoy participating in that," you realize you are operating outside of your Dot Life.

The first step required in eliminating something from our lives is to make ourselves aware of its presence. There are various things that can indicate why your life is always chaotic; let us take a look at a few of them.

YOU REFUSE TO BELIEVE THAT YOU HAVE A CHOICE

Believing that chaos is just a part of life and there is nothing you can do about it might be one of the reasons why your life is always full of chaos. Chaos doesn't happen on its own, in fact, it requires some action on your part for it to occur. Instead of having conscious control of the chaotic things happening around you, you just let them continue to happen unconsciously.

We need to stop believing that we don't have the ability to create our reality. We all possess the ability to create our own reality, and it happens through our thoughts.

YOU ONLY SPEAK ABOUT YOUR MISFORTUNES

If, whenever you get the chance to communicate with someone, you talk only about your misfortunes, this could be a reason there is chaos in your life. You need to realize that by focusing only on the negative aspects of your life, you are neglecting the positive things.

This can relate to feeling that you never have the energy to improve on manifesting your Dot Life—because you are fixated on the things that should have been removed in the first place. Your communication patterns follow the negative energy you embrace from media and people in your life. By allowing your Dot Life to be consumed in this way, you leave no room for positive, uplifting goals and actions.

You must remove your negative noise in order to fully engage in your positive dot. The Dot Life you live cannot be consumed by distractions of any kind. As you chip away these negative things, you understand better what positive energy feels like. You begin to look at misfortunes as opportunities for a positive outcome.

I took my misfortune during the real estate crash and focused on specific real estate goals and target growth markets and followed unreliable trends in real estate that were more risk adverse. My Dot Life-focused approach today positions me to further withstand extreme changes in the market. I have more focus on investments in positive and negative market volatility.

The goal here is to minimize, if not eliminate, all discussion and thought that reflects on negative events in your life. Use your misfortunes to strengthen your Dot Life goals.

CHAPTER FOUR

SOCIAL CHAOS
MANAGING DISORDER

In my late twenties and early thirties, my social life consisted of trying to fit in with every group I had ever associated with in one way or another. I have social groups that include various school mates, previous sport teams, coaching, the DJ music community, fraternity organizations, family, community, and professional business associates—to name a few.

Trying to keep up a calendar for all of these social interactions—coupled with my immediate family demands and involvement with society as a whole—was overwhelming, but I did not realize that early on in my life.

With my schedule so full, and with meeting so many expectations and demands in my social life, I began to realize that I was also forming unhealthy habits as I neglected important responsibilities. My weight ballooned from 205 to 225 in my mid-thirties. My clothing size went from L to XXL for some items. This was also when I learned that I was diabetic.

A little later, in my mid to late thirties, as I recapped that period of my life, I realized that eating without discipline had taken a toll on me. The combination of issues I was facing was a result of trying to live out my social connections through eating out, getting takeout, inviting friends over for get-togethers, and attending all kinds of functions. In addition to food there was always a drink or two to be had as well.

Separately, these events appear innocent, but together the mix created damaging results. My social chaos had also contributed to my unhealthy marriage and legal issues resulting from a DUI when returning from a function. My inability to focus and prioritize my social activities truly awakened me to the fact that I needed to make drastic changes to bring a sense of peace and calm to my life.

Thank God social media was not as prevalent when I reached age 30 as it is today. The complexity of trying to stay on top of everything that was going on around me socially limited my attention to detail in any of it. I was only touching the surface of things and could embrace or appreciate nothing. Everything was a passing event that satisfied the palate of my existence. There was no substance in anything I was doing.

Nothing added any true value that was rewarding or satisfying. The sheer number of things I chose to try to manage socially—never mind all the other distractions that also surrounded me—became one big ball of stress that cost me the ability to create a more stable foundation for navigating life.

If any of this sounds familiar, the goal here—as I

eventually learned—is to realize that you must find your Dot Life to truly weed out the unimportant things that block you from the things that matter.

A life that is fueled by social chaos typically includes the following elements:

NEGATIVE MEDIA

A simple definition of this term is: Information that is harmful to a person's reputation. This is a common occurrence in today's world of social media activity. There is a plethora of negative media out there that can dampen anyone's day. This kind of environment will seep into the well-being of the individual or group that is facing the negativity. Reputations are torn down and chaos is born, sometimes in the form of lawsuits or retaliatory media.

I used to drift toward reading media headlines when things were not going as well as I wanted—for comfort. What I mean is that we often find comfort in misery and negative information that aligns with our issues.

Today, I look for solutions to problems and connect with powerful examples of overcoming obstacles. In facing adversity and diving into solving problems, we provide ourselves with direct resolution plans instead of delaying issues and adding to our prolonged stress.

NEGATIVE ROLE MODELS

In a society such as ours with a proliferation of "influencers," there are multiple negative influences and role models that impact the people who look up to them in a negative way.

For instance, in our current bitcoin era, where cryptocurrency is the New Age mode of financial investment, role models have sprung up in every influencer camp, suggesting their knowledge or expertise on investing in cryptocurrencies—and encouraging anyone who follows them to take part in the risky investing positions they suggest. The crash of FTX is a gleaming example. Sam Bankman-Fried ran the empire that collapsed, losing billions of dollars that belonged to its investors. Many people had flocked to this blockchain technology without understanding the currency.

The result of much "influencer advice" can be detrimental for the people who believe and follow it. They introduce chaos in their lives by failing to understand the subject that they are engaging in and blindly following someone who they believe in.

A perfect circle of life does not have such chaos.

NEGATIVE FRIENDS

"Show me who your friends are, and I will tell you who you are."

This adage was expressed in the novel *Don Quixote* in the early 1600s, but it's even older than that, maybe stretching back to ancient times. It speaks to the reality of people's condition. A person is only as good as the company they keep. Negative company invariably means negative experiences. A friend who leads another into drug use—an activity that leads to deterioration of the mind and other aspects of life—is a negative friend.

I began to focus on the people around me and to take more concern for their interests and well-being. That provided me with a personal approach toward being what I consider a positive rather than a negative friend. I looked in a mirror first to make sure I was a positive influence. I realized that if I am not willing and able to provide a positive influence, I couldn't expect the same from them.

POOR COMMUNICATION TOPICS

We sometimes fail to engage in the right kind of communication that will lead us toward progressive paths. Just as having negative friends will cause chaos in our lives, habitually immersing ourselves in topics that have no hope or future for taking us toward our goals and positive achievement is a waste of valuable time. A result of chaos may be inevitable.

NEGATIVE ASSOCIATIONS

Negative associations can appear in many different forms. They appear when you become a chameleon, wanting and striving for things that ultimately don't truly matter; using the excuse of social distancing during the pandemic era of 2020 to embrace your comfort level of staying in unproductive negative situations; addiction to failure-related situations; participating in miscellaneous negative outings and events; shallow communication with friends and associates. All these and more represent negative associations. They take an emotional toll, leaving you unable to be or know yourself in social settings. One way to combat this is to turn down or stop engaging in miscellaneous lunches or dinners or outings that offer no positive interaction.

Here are a few other ways we create social chaos in our lives:

- Trying to impress others.
- Adapting to how others choose to live—by not having goals or a foundation of your own.
- Accepting and adopting others' ideas of home—by not having your own ideology of what makes you happy.

Notice when you do these things and the disorder they create in your life.

HOME CHAOS

Chaos can erupt in a person's home life in multiple ways. For context, home life represents that place where you live alone or with family or roommates. What are some of the things that can disrupt a life in the home, preventing you from realizing the perfect Dot Life? Here are a few:

- Living in an uncomfortable environment instead of changing it up, due to fear of change.
- Possessing so many physical things that nothing adds value anymore.

- Never understanding the real purpose of having a home fit for your children and family.
- Settling on sharing space with others, such as roommates, for the wrong reasons.
- Not focusing on the interests of your significant other and children.
- Failing to live in a setting that is geared toward partners' goals. A very prevalent problem can be found in the inability to track spending, thereby leading to money problems within the home.

MATERIAL THERAPY

Material therapy is not as complicated as it sounds. It refers to purchasing anything or everything to mask unhappiness within the home, or as a means of "Band-Aiding" emotional problems. It can also appear as following the trends and habits of others—the influencers—to create one's happiness as opposed to pursuing your own true happiness and goals.

MY HOME STORY

Through engaging Dot Life theories, my search for happiness has led me to different avenues for finding peace outside the box of my earlier negative outlets.

In my late twenties, thirties, and early forties, I used to have various avenues of escaping my reality and the lack of peace I constantly experienced in my chaotic world. I would turn to shallow outlets such as alcohol consumption, meaningless companionships, negative media consumption, and negative social interactions. I decided to remove these things that grounded me in a comfortable but negative environment. As I began to exercise this practice of removing negative influences, it forced me to focus on my home life and to evaluate what I was missing and why I was not satisfied.

In looking back, I had never been one to settle on anything I was enthusiastic about or to give full focus to things I believed in. I was always distracted by one thing or another. This included participation in sports, relationships, hobbies, and goals.

As a kid, I was focused on music and sports. I was considered talented in several sports and my hobby in music provided me with an opportunity to take my talents outside of my comfort zone—to hone my skills and perform locally.

In sports, I also had opportunities to take my talents outside the confines of my comfortable environment. But instead of nurturing my various aspirations, I focused only on basketball and gave up DJ-ing and football and baseball, which seemed like distractions from basketball. Then I eventually stopped playing basketball too, to pursue more creative interests.

I love to create and discover new things; however, I never had the attention span to remain committed to completing my new projects or sticking with them. I always moved on to the next new, shiny thing before completing the cycle of the current one. This is why I have lived in multiple homes, had multiple companions, owned more than 50 cars, traded out material items after material items, and, in general, started many things without finishing them.

My home was simply a place to be at that time. It was not a true home because it was filled with so many distractions and a lack of peace.

Stripping away the distractions from my home allowed me to truly focus on the core issues that were plaguing me. What were the distractions I needed to eliminate so that I could, at last, start focusing on a perfect life? I mentioned them earlier: alcohol consumption, meaningless companionships, negative media consumption, and negative social interactions.

Dropping these negative habits pulled away the layers of excuses, distractions, and misguided blame that I placed on others around me. A favorite quote from a good friend of mine that has resonated with me for years led me to understand where I am today. It was a conversation that ended with him asking me: "Have you ever taken the time to think that maybe it's you?" In other words, could I be the reason behind my own life's chaos?

This question from my good friend derived from a conversation we were having regarding relationships with friends and significant others. My home had always been a place of tension and anger. A lot of it was my inability to understand that my life and surroundings were driven by negative influences.

I started by removing the negative influences outside my home. One example of such negative influences would be chaotic spending habits and following negative media. As those negative forces peeled away outside my home, I began to recognize the numerous distractions within my home that also distorted my happiness. I decided to remove all the visual distractions—trinkets, pictures, refrigerator magnets, and even furniture that served no real purpose.

As the negatives began to peel away, I realized I did not miss any of my chaotic life. I also realized I enjoyed my home space with less stuff in it. It made me yearn for more of this new reality of having less. I removed the restrictions of living in an uncomfortable space and so many other negative habits that I had surrounded myself with for years. It made me desire to know where my true happiness lies.

It has become my obsession to positively disrupt the chaos in my environment and minimize my home surroundings, truly focusing on what I need to feed my happiness and creativity.

JOB / BUSINESS CHAOS

In the business world, chaos is a fixed feature. Most individuals would attest to the fact that their jobs and careers or businesses are chaotic. They certainly are not experiencing the perfect Dot Life in their businesses. Here are two of the chaotic business practices that we must deal with:

- Having unsuccessful people as role models.
- Doing business for personal gain only.

UNSUCCESSFUL BUSINESS MODELS

Following a business model that is doomed to fail from the beginning is what you want to avoid at all costs. Take the time to fully investigate your path to your business goals. Understanding that difference was a huge part of my business transformation, taking me from trying to manage as many projects as I could to focusing on analyzing profitability with fewer overall project totals.

Removing the following unsuccessful models has led me to my Dot Life goals in business:

- Following influencers as mentors who provide only the illusion of success, stability, and power. I was fortunate to experience both aggressive and conservative ownership structures, on a high level, at a young age. I was entrenched in the success illusion (aggressive) style of ownership and was able to witness the other from afar.
- Following a spend-first model to success instead of a wealth-first approach.
- Believing in the You Only Live Once model (YOLO), therefore spending before you earn.
- Engaging in unwise short-term business practices due to availability of capital for such practices.
- Forecasting next deals as the saviors of current unsuccessful deals.

- Not following your gut to work hard at being ahead of the curve while creating and innovating.
- Living in a spend-first justification culture that stifles creative growth and innovative ideas to advance.
- Pleasing others / finding self-satisfaction in negative ways that prevent growth and creative advancement.
- Creating negative relationships through the inability to show others a stable entry into business opportunities.
- Surrounding yourself with unsuccessful, unqualified people in the hopes of financial gains and the comfort of feeling superior in business situations.
- Not learning or growing your knowledge.
- Fear of releasing what is easy and taking risks for improvement.
- Engaging in work that is uncreative and uninspiring.
- Constantly battling the do-it-yourself model vs. hiring professionals to do their jobs.
- Failing to surround yourself with people who understand success and who have outcomes they are striving to achieve.

In working to survive, people constantly engage in scenarios that keep them rooted in never pursuing other options. They become tied to a system that they do not enjoy. They allow distractions to keep them from improving their situation.

RELATIONSHIP CHAOS

Relationships are inherently chaotic. I removed many friendship rituals in my mid-thirties that included time spent at social gatherings and drinking outings that did not promote positive goals and actions in my life. Instead, they caused me to ignore critical home duties as a husband and father in trying to juggle it all. To expect peace in relationships requires dedication in valuing your time and goals and how to maintain a Dot Life free of chaos.

In a marriage, you surely have moments of chaos. Of course, under normal circumstances, disagreements come to an end after each person decides they can reach a resolution. I realized my marriage was in chaos and began removing things that had to be removed to alleviate it. In all of my relationships I decided to look into the things I could do that would help to minimize chaos.

There are relationships that are perpetually unrestful. I have some personal favorites that are hallmarks of the experiences I had in the relationship segment of my imperfect non-Dot Life. Here are just a few relationship-chaos problems that I have experienced in the past:

- Getting into relationships to satisfy temporary happiness needs.
- Engaging in relationships due to shallow physical attraction only.

- Having a lack of authenticity with the relationship partner.
- Overlooking things that don't agree with your conscience or goals.
- Never having goals or standards for what you need and demand in relationships—ignoring your gut / happiness.
- Ignoring your inability to meet the goals of your partner.
- Having the wrong mindset: infidelity is normal, arguments are expected, working constantly to improve is not necessary.
- Having an inability to work for joint goals, values, and objectives.
- Not understanding that marriage / partnerships are top priority and everything else will fall in place behind it.
- Creating and/or falling into a comfort zone of accepting behaviors that are contrary to your goals or beliefs.
- Having bad examples to look up to in relationships.
- Masking the unhappiness in the relationship and presenting a false narrative to people.
- Lacking truthfulness with your partner, for instance, accepting the breaking of goals and rules in the relationship.
- Finding outlets to fulfill your wants and desires for temporary satisfaction while not being willing to work on the current relationship.

- Not being willing to have meaningful, engaging communication to constantly improve and strengthen the relationship.
- Lacking real intimacy in your home.
- Displaying vindictive and stubborn behavior with your partner.
- No willingness to plan or set joint goals.

Relationships are important in your Dot Life. Trying to maintain too many relationships vaguely—without true attachment—is a waste of time. Learn to cherish and support the relationships that are important to you and that provide value to others' Dot Life as well.

YOU ARE SCARED OF MOVING FORWARD

We tend not to dream big because we are too scared of failure and chaos. If you are someone who fears failing, then this might be the reason you are surrounded only by chaos. You need to recognize your fears and then slowly work toward how to overcome them. It might seem hard at first, but gradually you will overcome your fears by letting go of the things that are holding you back.

My earlier example regarding my involvement in sports provides another look at my decisions not to accept the challenge to excel at things I was considered above average in. Either I did not possess the grit to work on improving my skills in sports or hobbies that would have provided me with the confidence to step into a bigger arena and explore the next level or I simply lost interest. Either way, my inability to remain dedicated to developing my skills for long periods of time has resonated in all areas of my life.

Moving forward has been an issue for me at specific points of my life's journey. I truly understand now that I allowed my chaotic existence to hamper my judgment regarding following through and executing to the finish.

"Chaos often breeds life, when order breeds habit."
—Henry Adams

Chaos is the reason we exhibit unpredictable behavior. It can also induce confusion and disorganization. This chaos induces our bad habits to occur more frequently. You need to first recognize what your habits are and determine which ones are good and which ones are bad.

Bad habits will consume your time, thoughts, and actions. They take away from your ability to create and achieve important goals. Bad habits also cause other bad actions to pop up and further disrupt positive behavior.

Once you have recognized your bad habits, it then becomes easier for you to take steps that will help you get rid of them. This circle of life needs to be transformed into the circle of control, which is the next stage of transitioning to a more ordered life.

CHAPTER FIVE

CIRCLE OF CONTROL
UNDERSTANDING YOUR INFLUENCE

Beginning this book by introducing you to examples of a chaotic life was an ideal place to start because we are, after all, taking a journey from chaos to Dot Life.

The natural next topic to discuss in this progression is control. Now that we have considered the chaos, what do we do to control it? Or, more accurately, what did I do? How did I find my chaos-control solution?

I call it the "circle of control." If a dot is a circle and I am touting the perfect circle that represents a chaos-free life, then to have perfect control means starting from a point of control and ending at a point of control—the archetypal circle.

In the first part of this book, I described the four main areas of chaos as Social, Home, Jobs, and Relationships. We will follow the same model in this chapter. How do you achieve a circle of control in your social life, your home, your job, and your relationships?

You need to realize that although it might not always be easy for you to control things around you, there is nothing in this world that humans can't do. You need to stay consistent and remain patient to see the outcome. After you have recognized what your circle of life is, you need to remind yourself that you have the ability to take control over things. An effective way in which you can change your habits is by setting up certain goals.

SETTING GOALS

In order to accomplish anything in life, you need to set goals. A goal gives you motivation and a purpose to remain consistent with what you are doing. A life without a goal is like living life without any purpose. It is almost like driving in an unknown city without having a map. A goal actually serves as a map for you. It provides you with the basic guidelines and things that you need to follow to accomplish your aim.

Here is how you can set goals to change your habits. There are a few steps involved: the first is to have a proper understanding of the goal you seek to achieve.

ANALYZE THE GOAL

To begin at the absolute starting point of goal setting, establish the purpose: ask yourself why you want to achieve this goal. For instance, let us assume that you want to achieve a goal of starting a business in addition to your day job. Ask yourself the question:

Why do I want to start a business?

Your answer might be, "Because I want to create

something that I care about instead of just doing a generic job."

Ask yourself another level of why questions: *Why do you think it is important to create a business you care about?*

Your answer might be: "It would mean I will be able to help people in a meaningful career."

Then ask yourself the next level of why: *Why is it important for you to hold this value of helping people?*

Your answer: "It would give me a selfless purpose for getting up and going to work every day."

You have analyzed your goal to a point where it has simplified the reason for your next steps.

When you are able to analyze your decisions before making them, it uncomplicates your life. It makes living just a little bit simpler.

MAP YOUR DIRECTION

Another necessity for the simplified life is a life of direction. It's admirable to know why you set a goal, but do you know which direction you should go in to drive that goal? Do you have, for example, a five-year plan for the business you have decided to set up—a plan that maps out where you want to be and what you hope to achieve in five years' time?

When you map out the direction to where you need to go in any situation, you have effectively simplified your life!

ESTABLISH CONTROL

Without a doubt, the world today spins out of control because of systems, processes, and even cultures that have been in existence for so long that societies do not want to deviate from them.

When you set goals for yourself, you are placing yourself in control. It is a way of announcing that regardless of limitations, systemic restrictions, or any other obstacle that may be in your way, you have created an environment where you are more likely than not to succeed.

Creating a well-rounded dot, devoid of distractions and risks, allows your control to be less dependent on social whims. You hear that stocks are taking a beating, the housing market is crashing, and food prices soaring, but a well-rounded Dot Life will position you to be affected minimally by the dramatic ups and downs.

I have made great strides toward minimizing my desire to acquire things and spend money frivolously. To establish that kind of control is to position yourself to be happy and stable most of the time. Your success can only truly be measured by what you determine it should be. What makes you happy is unique to you.

MAKE IT S.M.A.R.T.

There is a well-publicized method that helps goal setters achieve their objectives in a controlled environment. The S.M.A.R.T. principle[1], introduced by George T. Doran in an issue of *Management Review*, is an acronym that describes the steps one needs to undergo in order to follow through on goals. It is all well and good to analyze, have direction, and establish control for your goals—but you need to become practical in implementing them. This is where the S.M.A.R.T. principle comes in. It means setting goals that are Specific, Measurable, Achievable, Relevant, and Time-bound.

Consider this process for any goal that you wish to achieve, and you will simplify your life in the process. Is the goal specific? A nebulous, undefined goal becomes messy and uncertain when you try to figure out the resources you will need and the commitments and other requirements that it may demand from you. Simply saying "I want to start a business" is going to make your life a little complicated. You need to be more specific so that you can embark on steps to attain your goal. For instance: I want to start an interior decorating business.

Is the goal measurable? In other words, how will you know when you have achieved it? Is there something specific about the interior design business that, once it occurs, would demonstrate to you that you have succeeded in what you set out to do? Let's assume that your benchmark of success is to earn $5,000 within the first two months of business. By setting such a measure in place, you have a determinable vision that you are pursuing, and it is contributing to your desired circle of life wherein your life is getting simpler.

Have you set a goal that is achievable? For instance, if you have determined that the business should earn $5,000 within two months of your setting it up, are you sure that you can achieve that, given, for instance, your skills, your environment, your access to clientele, and other factors that will play into determining how much money you can earn? An achievable goal is a simplified goal.

Another step to life simplification in goal setting is to ensure that you understand your goals. At the beginning of this section, there was an exercise about asking yourself "why" multiple times to arrive at the root reason that you are embarking on any mission. Figuring this out will simplify the objective because a well-defined aim is an aim that will typically enjoy motivation.

Finally, a time-bound goal is a life-simplifying goal! Imagine enrolling at a university for a degree, but not having a set timeline for when you will complete your studies! Throughout history, this has led some students to spending upward of eight years—maybe even 10—in a single degree area of study!

Deciding that you will earn $5,000 within two months is a good example of a time-bound goal. You have identified a timeline for achieving something specific and you begin to expend your resources for the achievement of that timeline.

In the subsections that follow, we will look at goal setting for a simplified life in a broader light to help you determine other factors to consider after you have set your goals.

DOT YOUR EXPECTATION OF WHAT MONEY SHOULD BRING YOU

You must laser focus on your need for money as it relates to your happiness. To dot that expectation is to recognize what it takes to make you feel that you are living life with no stress.

1. Know what makes you happy, not what money can buy you.

The goal is not to make money and be successful just to give it all to someone else. Many people feel that money is created and earned for the purpose of purchasing all the material things and pleasures that life has to offer. Many people celebrate their wealth by enjoying all things afforded that way. Living an unhealthy lifestyle and chasing instant gratification typically turns out badly for most people. Your lifestyle choice should not be dictated by how much you can afford but what fulfills the areas in your dot that make you happy. Having an understanding of what you require for happiness within your dot provides a level of awareness as to how little money dictates happiness.

2. Each goal breeds a new goal that does not fit in your Dot Life.

When reaching success on a financial goal, many people marry this with goals for obtaining new things. These things were typically outside of your dot goals when finances were not available. Creating a plan and budget is crucial to living within your dot. If there is no dot plan, there is no way to know your limits and have control over keeping your dot healthy.

3. Be wary of Dot Life expansion creep.

Have you ever found yourself making purchases with the excuse that "you earned it" or "I will replace something else I have when I get home." This is my definition of Dot Life expansion creep. Your perfect collection of dots that form the picture you want to see of yourself will start to have bulges and blemishes as the microdots and negative habits increase. Be sure to stay firm on the things you need vs. the things that bring no value to your life. Dot expansion creep starts the chain reaction to debt, stress, and chaos that drains you of your time and finances.

Going on vacation always brought on the need for me to purchase "vacation clothes" for the trip. Ironically, while on that vacation, I also felt the need to purchase clothes. This is another example of Dot Life expansion creep. The need to shop on vacation is something I now have given up. I have conditioned myself to focus completely on where I am going and the cultural experience. I have no interest in shopping—wasting time and taking away from that experience. The first thing I used to look for while on vacation was the nearest mall or outlet. Even before getting there, my focus was buying vacation shirts, shoes, and new swimwear to complete the intended journey. While reducing the need for this activity, I also began to focus on my needs while packing. The amount of luggage was reduced, the time preparing for trips was reduced, and more time was focused on the actual experience.

4. Do not reward yourself for achieving Dot Life goals with non-Dot Life rewards. Reward yourself by strengthening another area inside your Dot Life.

An option to making non-productive purchases is to take a positive financial win and apply it to another area within your Dot Life that strengthens you even more. When I paid off all my debt, I celebrated my future financial gains by applying that planned income to additional savings and investment goals outside of my budgeted amounts. What I realized was that once the right mindset is achieved, it creates a chain reaction of positive decision-making, even outside of the original goals. It became an obsession to continue to achieve goals and apply them in other areas that increase time in my life and decrease my stress level even further.

5. Keep your Dot Life fun and pleasurable.

Keeping things in your life that you genuinely enjoy is what I consider "Premium Minimalism." These are the areas in your life that involve the things you genuinely enjoy and have a passion for. This is the area within your Dot Life that you have identified as where you want to use your time.

When I identify the things I truly enjoy, places I want to see, and simply do things that I find intriguing at any given moment, that is what I want my Dot Life to be. This lifestyle that I enjoy consists of things that make me happy and not what someone else thinks should make me happy. This is where I focused on removing all expenses that drained my budget but brought me no real pleasure or had no purpose. Once I let go of the many things I wasted money and time on, I focused on creating and enjoying the best experiences I could. I also decided to take mini vacations to relax and focus on my mental and physical health.

HAVE YOUR OWN REASON

You need to have a reason you are willing to change this habit of yours. This will remind you of why you are changing your habits in the first place. It could be that you want to stop binge eating so that you can avoid health problems such as obesity or heart disease. It could be the reason you are willing to quit smoking—because you want to live a healthier lifestyle and avoid health problems in the future.

You also need to feel ready to accept the change. It is okay to take time, but it's necessary to make a plan for yourself. Once you are ready, then the next step for you is to start setting up the goals.

SET GOALS THAT YOU CAN REACH

You need to set smart goals for yourself. This means that if your long-term goal is to lose weight, then you need to develop certain short-term goals to achieve the long-term. In this way, it becomes easier for you to keep up with the progress, and it also keeps you motivated to do it. Here is how to develop your plan of goals:

Long-Term Goals: These are the goals that you are aiming to achieve in a year or three years or five years, and so on.

Short-Term Goals: These are the goals that you are aiming to achieve daily, weekly, monthly, or in six months.

Updated Goals: It is equally important for you to stay updated on your goals so that you can track your progress. This will also tell you if you need to make any adjustments to the plan.

Stay focused more on the smaller goals because achieving them will take you closer to your ultimate big goal. Another important way to stay consistent with your goals is by writing them down, which helps plant them in your memory.

Updating your goals (weekly) keeps you focused on your Dot Life plan as well as providing you with motivation to stay on task and not drift into negative influences / habits.

As an example, think of going grocery shopping without a list of the things that you want—there is a good chance you might forget a thing or two. So, to remain consistent with your goals, be sure to write them down on a piece of paper and place it somewhere you will see it and be reminded easily. You might even make a vision board related to your goal.

Be sure that whatever goals you set for yourself are specific. In this way, you are better able to achieve them. For example, writing "eat four fruits a day" is better than writing "eat more fruit." This helps you to accomplish your goal faster.

When you are trying to accomplish goals, assess each goal separately. Focus solely on one goal at a time. Once you have accomplished your goal, give yourself a reward to celebrate your new behavior. After that, you can focus on accomplishing your next goal.

REDUCING BAD HABITS

Here is a breakdown of how you can reduce your unhealthy habits:

Finding the Cue (Why did you make this bad decision?)

This is the first step in reducing a bad habit. For this reason, you need to write down at least five events that made you want to engage in that negative behavior. After writing those things down, you will have more clarity about the reasons you got started on it—the time of day, what happened prior to it, and whether anyone else was involved.

Identifying the Reward

You might not immediately be able to identify the value or reward you get from getting rid of negative behavior. Think about it; identify whether there is an immediate reward or if it will manifest over time. You can then try to adjust your routine to see if you recognize the feeling that the reward gives you. Does it provide you with extra energy? Does it relieve your stress? Be open to the answer.

The reward of having my mind clear to explore my creative space is the best of all rewards for me. I have more time to solve issues, design, write, and make better decisions. I can think through these things effectively and efficiently.

Start with Something Small

Change does not happen overnight. Millionaires don't become millionaires in the span of a day. Change requires dedication, hard work, and consistency that brings us closer to our goals. To break your bad habit, you need to first start with something small. You need to become more aware of what you are doing. Cleaning out one room in your house and realizing the peace it brings you will motivate you to tackle more areas in your home.

Observe What You Get

After you can recognize what your unhealthy habits are, find a connection between those actions and the actions that lead to the outcome. Your sensations are linked with the way you feel certain things.

With every action that you take, there is a certain sensation attached to it. You need to recognize the sensation it gives you. For example, if you are trying to quit smoking, then you need to ask yourself about the kind of sensations that smoking gives you: what it tastes like, what it smells like, what feeling it produces inside you. You will then realize that smoking might not be that pleasing to your senses. This is how to pay attention to what is happening in the present moment. This will also change your perspective about things that you once found pleasurable.

SOCIAL CONTROL

We have talked about the negative aspects of our society: poor communication and negativity among friends, bad media, and a variety of other unconstructive social outlets. How do you exit the chaos that this negativity causes? Here are some tactics:

- Create Minimalist Goals: Start a reduction of all things negative. Reduce social media time, remove purchase goals, reduce your eating-out budget to specific dates and times.
- Reduce your daily social media interaction or use.
- Reduce and set specific times when you view social media, talk to socially negative people, and take refuge in negative social activities.

- Create self-check reflection points throughout the day.
- At the end of each day, reflect on all negative social interactions you were compelled to gravitate toward.
- Start understanding the reasons you gravitate toward those things and determine how they massage your comfort of unhappiness and goal setting.
- Recognize the stifling effect those things have on your overall happiness.
- As you challenge yourself to reduce some social interactions, exchange them for positive goals and interests that you wish to take their place.
- Start researching positive / interesting people and topics.
- Start evaluating the people around you who do not promote the positive goals and interests needed to improve you.
- Stop trying to find situations you deem worse than yours to create a temporary comfort in your unhappiness.
- Finding comfort in negative stories and sad situations will only prolong and deepen your unhappiness and motivation to do better and achieve happiness / confidence.

HOME

Filling your home with the empty presence of material possessions to replace the void of emptiness is not an effective strategy for achieving peace. I would know—I tried it. I had to have any and every trinket within my home confines: vases, fake flowers, picture frames, trophies, etc. were everywhere. If your home is filled with comfort items that give you the illusion of happiness, it is time to evaluate the importance and need of having "stuff." In my usual bullet point fashion, I will list what I discovered about my own materialism mentality and what to do about it.

Ask yourself these questions:

- What is the purpose of owning a multitude of clothing, shoes, gadgets, or furniture?
- Why do we need a bigger home, oversized cars, luxury cars, luxury purses, luxury watches?
- Who are we looking to satisfy with things that create dread and unhappiness once the newness wears off?

Think about these points:

- We follow and strive to live the life of illusion we see on social media and in media itself that provides constant imagery of high-end living / purchasing / happy moments / celebrations, etc.

- We tend to ignore the eventual removal / selling off or falling off of many people in the cycle.
- We are blinded by the constant need to be "up on the latest" in technology, fashion, or cars.

Make these steps:

- Complete an evaluation of things to start the process of understanding what's important and what needs to be eliminated from your home.
- Removing stuff that is not needed will help clear your mind of clutter you don't realize exists.
- Resolve issues of credit card debt, repair bills, and other expenses that cloud your ability to explore and achieve positive outlooks and outcomes.

Getting rid of things is extremely hard in the beginning but extremely rewarding once you get past starting the process. You really start to question everything you purchase or consider purchasing going forward.

Once you remove the need to consume "things," you move into the need to reduce financial obligations. Of course, I am referring to the credit card debt, subscriptions, or bad purchase habits.

Start by removing any credit options. One famous

practice I think should be adopted by anyone who wants to get out of debt: cut up your credit cards.

As your spending decreases, the consequential result will be that you will clearly have more funds to spend on debt repayment.

Consider a debt consolidation option. This will remove the constant clutter of various bills, obligations, or commitments. Set timelines for getting out of debt and set financial goals for what you will do with the money. Stick to your goals as they are extremely important to this process.

So many people are silently stressed by an overwhelming number of bills appearing monthly from various creditors. We pay the minimums, but the process leads us to worrying, drinking, and other pacifiers to get through it—never solving the problem but just moving us through until the next cycle. Debt consolidation provides one bill and clarity for you to investigate ways to accelerate eliminating your debt. Once this is achieved, your consumption habits will become strategic and effective, wherein money spent is based on careful planning.

JOB / BUSINESS

If you are unhappy at work, it could be due to a number of reasons: you are not making enough money; you are not enthusiastic about creating something rewarding; you find that you can't focus on changing anything. If these things are true for you, it is time to remove the chaos and find the time to determine and achieve clarity on what you intend to do with your career.

A job will be just a job if it is constantly tied to achieving social and consumer goals that are unhealthy and negative. When a person is trying to increase income solely with the goal of increasing purchasing habits and obtaining bigger homes and cars, they will only end up in what we call "advanced unhappiness."

CREATE YOUR GOALS IN THE FOLLOWING AREAS

Savings: How do I eliminate unnecessary costs to save?

- Focus on reducing the time spent on chasing non-productive avenues. It is unfortunate that people chase careers without full focus on being the best they can be in their market.
- Take steps to achieve your highest and fullest potential by creating a couple of high-value goals and eliminate your lesser goals until those of high-value are achieved.
- Realize your true passion and setup your one-, three-, and five-year goals to turn that passion into income.
- Adjust your focus areas to zero in on those goals that have a defined "why." Why are you doing this, what is your end plan for this goal?
- If your lifestyle is causing you to incur debt, you may find that you must engage in jobs that you dislike to afford that life. Reassess your lifestyle and why it is necessary to engage

in those things that are making you spend. When you realize that freedom is better than the hole of being tied to doing something you do not love—just for money—it will be a liberating journey to exit it!

- Your passion should drive your goals. Don't focus on the outcome (money, fame, etc.), focus on your enjoyment of the journey to your goals.
- Your job and side hustles should be set up to reach your goals and objectives and to provide you with the means to achieve your full-circle potential.
- Start breaking down what you are doing currently to eliminate non-productive processes and distractions that do not align with your passion and targets.
- Stay focused on your objectives.

RELATIONSHIPS

Relationships are imperative as a focus when you are building a life where discipline and harmony are primary features. In the past, my perspective on how to approach a relationship was by way of my goals and desires; my focus was not on the relationship itself but what I received from it. I felt that if I provided what I perceived my partner needed from me they should be happy. I have since learned and understood that everyone has their own interpretation of what is important to them and that communication is required to nurture and understand that.

I will outline five segments of relationships that I believe should be the principal focus when you are trying to attain a circle of control.

Marriage / Partner Segment

Are you prepared to share your life with a partner in marriage?

Many individuals tend to get into a marriage relationship merely due to societal pressure. They were not ready to settle and give up their independence, but they did it anyway because the community around them made them believe that it was time.

This can create fertile ground for resentment between the marriage partners. They resent each other for the time they could have spent away from each other. The end result is sometimes separation or divorce.

There are also marriage relationships that grow chaotic simply because the partners did not settle down to understand each other's dos and don'ts or their particular personalities.

Your relationship situation is unique. It's not possible to list all the various nuances that might cause chaos within it, but in general, the recommendation is to assess your marriage, determine what is causing the chaos, and decide on how to resolve it.

Family Segment

We all grew up in our individual families. They nurtured and fed us and taught us our first life lessons. Yet the reality is that not all family members represent a positive influence in our lives.

Your assignment, in getting rid of a chaotic family situation, is to determine the family members with whom you must establish positive nurturing relationships, and work hard at doing so. These family members might include your wife or husband, children or stepchildren, your father and mother, and ideally your in-laws as well.

Friends Segment

To drive chaotic friendships out of your life, determine which of your positive input to your goals and needs. Understand and ascertain your ability to provide the same for them. Eliminate all others that have had a negative impact on you or your positive goals in the past. (The operative word here is "positive.")

Business Segment

Once you establish your business targets, you must initiate the required relationships to achieve them. These include relationships with mentors, coaches, and business partners or employees.

Eliminate all negative, non-productive, and non-motivated people from your business associations. I established a bad habit of looking for the best deal while ignoring the value of customer service and professionalism. This created a lot of stress and heartache in managing these negative situations.

Social Segment

Social interaction needs to be calculated, purposeful, positive, and motivating. Start your social growth and eliminate chaos by not accepting invitations or associations with people who have no proof that their work supports the goals you seek to attain. For instance, if you want to be a copywriter and you are looking for a copywriter mentor, choosing one who does not have proof of clients served and satisfied is not an ideal association for the target you seek to attain.

After identifying the chaos around you and assessing how to put it under control, the next phase of your dot journey is to begin putting the perfect circle of life in place! Now, we begin part three of the journey—The Dot Life and how to achieve it.

FINDING A BETTER OFFER

The Dot Life is an improved offer. You need to find a reward for yourself that is more rewarding than the existing one that your mind is used to. The reason your brain is addicted to the older habit is that it believes it is already receiving its bigger and better reward. The trick here is to convince your brain that there is a reward that is *way* bigger and better than the current one.

Today, there is one thing that everyone has access to —technology. There are more than a hundred apps that can help you to overcome your bad habits. You need to focus more on mindfulness training apps such as Headspace that will help you realize that a reward of a good and ordered life is better than a temporary coping mechanism.

It is true that the reason we fall into bad habits is that we don't know other ways to cope with our problems. Gradually, with time, you come to the realization that there is always a bigger and better reward.

This is how to manage the circle of control. You can control your life, and it is never too late to make a change in your life. After learning how to be in control of your actions, the next step is to shift toward the Dot Life. This is the stage where you will become aware of what new things you should add to your routine and how to remain consistent with this new positive habit of yours.

CHAPTER SIX

DOT LIFE

GETTING INTO IT

The time is now to move into your Dot Life and embrace all that it has to offer. My embracing it has allowed me to truly understand what's important and to stay completely motivated to continue to fight off negativity. My goals in life remain focused on creating a stress-free and minimalist environment. I can recall the weight lifted off me once I grasped the notion that material items were taking up my time here on Earth. I truly felt the weight lifting off me as my process of digging into a successful Dot Life brought me the excitement not only of living it but also sharing it with the people around me.

Fulfilling my Dot Life goals and living the system turned me into a role model as more and more people began to express their desire to get help with their journey in the process. I am embracing that leadership more and more and becoming more vocal in expressing myself while helping others live a better life. Take a close look at the following chapters for an in-depth journey into ways to get started in different areas of your life. Your Dot Life needs to reflect how you live now and your plans for future lifestyle projections as well.

When you are transitioning from your old lifestyle, it is important to shift to a more minimalist style. This is the next big step after you have trained your brain on how to get rid of old habits that are bad for your health. You need to find a new self-focus that will keep you on the right track. You need to make sure that you eliminate all the negative influences that are making you constantly fall back to your unhealthy habits.

MINIMALIST LIFE SYSTEM

Minimalism[1] is not a new concept: a lot of people have been practicing this lifestyle for quite a long time. It is the simplest way of living, and it helps you to declutter the areas of your life that bring you negative energy.

Minimalism also has deep roots historically. It is the chosen way of a Buddhist[2] life, shun whatever materialistic possessions that one has. This gained the attention of the world in the 20th century.

The Definition of Minimalist

The main idea of minimalism is to focus on the things that really matter—and that means eliminating all the stuff that does not bring you internal happiness. It is entirely up to you how you choose to live with fewer things. You live your life based on experiences rather than materialistic possessions. It gives you an opportunity to spend more time with the people you love.

The Benefits of a Minimalist Lifestyle

There are several advantages associated with a minimalist way of living. Let us take a look at how this simple lifestyle can provide us with benefits:

- It helps you to declutter the stuff that is irrelevant. You are aware that things do not add value to your life, so you get rid of them.
- It helps you focus more on your priorities, which brings you closer to your goals.
- It saves you from debt, which saves you from getting stressed over financial matters.
- It relieves you from all kinds of unnecessary stress, and it promotes a supportive attitude and feeling.
- When you rid your home of extra stuff, you are better able to manage stress because, according to a study held in 2011, it has been proven that clutter has the ability to increase your cortisol level. Cortisol is the hormone that is responsible for increasing stress.

Things to Do

Here are some of the things that you need to do for a minimalist lifestyle:

- If you have fewer things, you can shift to a smaller place. This can save you a lot of money as it will require fewer utilities.
- Extra bills can make budgeting extremely hard, so be sure to eliminate unnecessary

expenses. Make every purchase purposeful. Make no purchase that can't be justified positively.

- Ensure that you are valuing experiences more than materialist things.
- Everything depends on your focus. As a part of the transitioning process, create a new self-focus.

CREATING A NEW SELF-FOCUS

Self-awareness is the most important thing for all individuals. It is like a mirror that gives you insights into your inner self. Every individual has two sides. One side is the one that they see every day in the mirror. The other side is their interior.

The principal things that matter are your thoughts and your feelings. When you provide the right kind of nourishment to your inside, you will see your outside flourishing on its own. It is important to see what is going on inside you every now and then. In that way, you get to know more about your strengths and your weaknesses.

LIMIT YOUR FOCUS

Multitasking can drain most of your energy and decrease your productivity, so you end up completing nothing. Focus on one thing at a time and be careful about which things you give your attention.

Your attention is like your spotlight, and wherever you shine it, it will highlight that spot. This is why it is important to pay attention to the things that induce positive behavior in you. If you spend a lot of time watching TV and reading non-productive blogs, you are giving away time and energy that could be providing peace of mind. I decided a long time ago to remove all unnecessary TVs from my home. I notice even today when visiting people, the first thing they do is turn on a TV. I know something I speak up about when it occurs. I politely request that it not be done or ask what the plan is for watching TV. Typically, they look at the remote and laugh.

Making too many scheduled and unscheduled commitments is another area that is an issue for me. I have had to personally decline routine outings that distracted from my overall focus and goals.

Reducing your Dot Life goals so that you can achieve them one at a time is an excellent way to stay focused. I have learned that trying to complete too many tasks at the same time spreads my capacity to truly complete what's important for the immediate goal too thin.

LIVE IN THE MOMENT

Focusing can turn out to be difficult if you are constantly thinking about things that happened in your past and worrying about things that have yet to happen. You need to learn to live fully in the present moment. This makes you more aware of every action that you take, and it gives you more control.

Instead of resenting your past, you need to focus on how you can make your present condition better. Your past does not define you, and your future has yet to come. Stay in the present moment so that you can aim for the best outcome. Be sure to engage in fewer distractions and focus on the things that will bring you closer to your goal.

ELIMINATING ALL NEGATIVE INFLUENCES

Once you have figured out which things are negative influences in your life, you need to eliminate all those influences. The types of people you surround yourself with matters a lot as well, and you need to be careful with that. In the past, I noticed my personality changing when around negative people and places. My demeanor changed as I became comfortable within those environments.

The best way to overcome negative influences that get in the way of your productivity is to change them into something positive.

TURNING NEGATIVE ENERGY INTO POSITIVITY

If your thoughts are constantly negative, it can be hard for you to maintain your focus on productive and positive things. This induces more worry, anxiety, and stress, which makes it harder for you to remain in the present moment. You need to turn this energy into something more positive. This can be as simple as taking a step away and going for a walk. Close your eyes for a few seconds and take deep breaths. This is a simple way to bring you to the present moment. Once you have calmed yourself, you can then proceed toward taking action. It's impossible to think straight when the mind and body are under extreme stress. Another technique is to write down the problem and then evaluate it so that you can find the right solution in an efficient manner. Taking a small break is important as it gives you some time away from worrying about things.

On that note, let us turn to looking at the various segments of your life where you can start implementing the Dot Life. The format will be the same as in the earlier chapters of this book. You want to focus on your Home, Family, Business, and Social Life as the centers where achieving a perfect-circle dot is necessary.

HOME

There are a few considerations when de-cluttering your home for Dot Life. How does the perfect Dot Life appear in your home? Let me count the ways.

- Reduce or eliminate all unnecessary knick-knacks.
- Remove all unproductive apps and programs from phones and computers.
- Consolidate all debt, remove all credit cards from daily access.
- Remove all non-productive subscriptions.
- Review and update all plans for monthly payments.
- Create plans for food consumption. The planning process will create a positive eating

experience at home and away from home. It will reduce your spending significantly and at the same time provide experiences you enjoy.

- Consider whether you have executed the Dot Life plan in all areas. This will ensure that your experiences with dining, home-meal planning, prep, and grocery shopping will improve. No longer are you eating unhealthily due to stress, or, if you are inclined to alcohol, drinking heavily to temporarily erase thinking about debt, stress, and problems due to poor planning.

Escapism is the worst way to approach activities like dining and vacations. It means escaping from your reality by taking a vacation or perhaps taking yourself out for an expensive, fine-dining experience. Remember Southwest's "Wanna get away" slogan? This was an advertisement for flight packages for mini vacations. I have learned that although you fly away to escape issues, it does nothing to eliminate the issues themselves upon return.

BUSINESS / JOBS

Remove all unproductive negative associates, contractors, businesses suppliers, etc. Review and remove all expenses not related to growth planning or production, evaluate staffing needs, job hours, personal hours, and project and training hours required to achieve your goals.

This phase—the Dot Life phase—requires tough decisions that go against most of what you were taught to believe. Our age of technology has significantly changed how business gets done. Business systems today require far less human interaction and processing steps to achieve goals. These changes are occurring extremely fast as technology is becoming more and more advanced. Focus on what you do and how you do it.

The Dot Life approach is going to help you eliminate antiquated processes that would be distractions in your progress.

RELATIONSHIPS

What are some of the Dot Life actions you can take in your relationships?

- Evaluate personal relationships and identify the positives and negatives of each.
- Determine whether your relationships are focused on improvement or whether it's time to let go. Advise relationship counterparts of expectations you have for them and give the same to them in return.
- Determine your initial small circle to start.
- Document the priority of each member in your inner circle. How important are they to you and how important are you to them?

SOCIAL

A couple of things to consider for your social media Dot Life are:

- Reduce social media to two 30-minute sessions a day.
- Stop all participation with negative, non-productive people in the media.

TRY HELPING OTHER PEOPLE

It is easier to be influenced by negative things and influences if you are extremely selfish. Step out and help other people. This will give you a sense of purpose and it will motivate you. It doesn't have to be something big; you can start with something small that might help someone. It can be as simple as asking someone about their day or holding the door for someone.

The point is to focus more on positive behavior and to focus less on things that bring up a negative influence on your life.

KNOW THAT YOU DO NOT KNOW IT ALL

It seems a very simple notion that when we don't know something, we should not create unnecessary stress in trying to act as though we do. This is a phenomenon that happens to most individuals. Maybe we all have a little of the "imposter syndrome" mindset. In a fight of wills, people have been known to pretend to have knowledge, abilities, or other capacities in areas that they actually do not. It is true that you don't need to be perfect in a particular skill area before embarking on it; however, being a newbie to an area of skill is one thing, touting that you have more knowledge about it than you actually do is yet another. It may be the reason there is a preponderance of "imposter syndrome" among many individuals today. Imposter syndrome, by definition, is a feeling of inadequacy about your skills and achievements and feeling that society will soon discover that you have been lying about your skills or qualifications or other things about yourself. And why wouldn't you feel inadequate if you are pretending to have knowledge that you do not?

For this reason, a Dot Life makes you truer to yourself. You will not embark on a stressful path of pretending to know something that you do not, because you are not only simplifying your life, but you're also simplifying your mind as well.

HAVE GUIDING PRINCIPLES FOR YOUR LIFE

Guiding principles, otherwise known as philosophy, will enable an individual to live a non-arbitrary life. At this point in this book, it should be obvious that the Dot Life concept is not just about simplifying your life, but about ensuring that the simple life is meaningful. When you develop a philosophy for your life, you are creating a "real" you. You have a focal point which, when other philosophies, ideas, or principles come your way and try to complicate your mind, allows you to know where you stand. You are able to remain simple and true to the principles you believe in.

MONEY RELATIONSHIP

Money makes the world go round. I make no pretenses in this book in regard to how essential money is for a Dot Life. You need money to live. In fact, it is one of the essential commodities that will make your life simpler. With money, you can rent or buy a home in the place you desire, eat the type of food you love, engage in the type of activities you like—all with ease of mind, knowing you can afford them instead of getting into overwhelming debt because of them.

For this reason, to live a Dot Life and simplify your existence, you need to consider your relationship with money. Does money control you or do you control it?

Make peace with money by understanding how to manage it in such a way that you are not living off credit cards and loans. The fact is the person who has less debt is the person who has more wealth.

You may be an individual who does not care about wealth building. You simply want to live the Dot Life that is discussed in this book. Maybe living off the grid is a goal for you so that you don't have to deal with utilities and financial systems.

But even a person who lives off the grid will have expenses from time to time. They may live completely off the land—their food, home, and other things they rely on may be "free." That is the ultimate simplified life.

Or is it?

Even a life off the grid will require resources that may require some money. The bottom line of having a good relationship with money—no matter the type of Dot

Lifestyle you adopt—is that it will see you on the road to a perfect Dot Life faster.

CONTENTMENT IS KEY

We live in a society where individuals—and businesses—compete. Competition is necessary in a capitalist society.

For a Dot Life, it is not.

Competition, in the midst of one's personal lifestyle, can be draining and unrewarding. While businesses do it to stay ahead of the game in their industries, an individual who wishes to adopt a Dot Life should engage in less competition—or none at all.

When you begin to understand that you are a unique individual with features that set you apart from everybody else, you will find that you have no need to prove yourself in regard to how you look or perform in the eyes of your peers. That is the bedrock of contentment—being satisfied with who you are and your lot in life. While there is room to achieve greater things, you are always content at whatever level you find yourself even as you aim for improvement.

IT'S ACCEPTABLE TO BE AVERAGE

In a society where we all grew up being told that we could be anything we want to be, it can be very disappointing to be mediocre at anything.

This is not to discredit the practice of parents encouraging their children to "reach for the stars" or "never settle for less" or any other excellence-invoking encouragement that parents give their children. However, having an excellence mentality does not mean we should be intolerant of the times we experience abasement.

A Dot Life is one that accepts mediocrity because it knows that it can also achieve excellence. While that is not an excuse to remain mediocre, it is a recognition that it is all right to be the average person in a group from time to time. It removes the need for competition or comparison with one's peers, a practice in our current society that causes untold emotional turmoil for many an individual.

The Dot Life recommends: Being average is all right.

MOMENTS OF STILLNESS

I am about to recommend something scandalous. Here it comes: *You don't have to be busy all the time. You can be still.*

The Dot Life, the simplified life, provides an opportunity for anyone to start connecting with their peaceful side. In a world of chaos, running around, and other distractions, the power to be still eludes many individuals, families, and households. There is always something to do, some place to be, and some "busyness" to get into.

As you build your Dot Life, the perfect life that has simplified things for you, get even simpler by learning the benefits of having intentional peaceful moments—or several of them—during the course of any day. With intent, take some time away and spend it at a quiet park, or, if you cannot get away from home, shut down all devices and gadgets and step away from people for a short while. Maybe close yourself off in a quiet room and take the time to simply decompress, or declutter your mind, or gather your thoughts. This can be instrumental to strengthening your mind and helping you develop the tenacity needed to continue with the life-simplification process—something that seems so counter-cultural that you will need all the courage you can muster to embark on it and continue to sustain it!

DO NOT BE A JACK OF ALL

One of the features of the modern age is that people are raised to be multi-taskers with the belief that they can be all things to all people and do all things at the same time.

This is not humanly possible.

In your newly adopted Dot Life, embrace the fact that you are, in fact, human. You cannot be all things to all people. Accept yourself, your flaws, and your weaknesses.

Understand that it is good to aim for the skies, but you can't be everything. This mindset will awaken your ability to focus. If you were, for instance, thinking of going into a graphic design plus marketing plus website-consultant type of business—which sounds like it's all the same artsy area, but it really isn't—don't. Somewhere along the line when you have worked in each discipline, one by one, and developed some degree of expertise in each area, you may consider branching out into an additional space. But not before. Don't stretch yourself thin by becoming a Jack. The Dot Life forbids it.

HAVE STANDARDS

How do you become a person with high standards? It is very simple:

Identify your boundaries—and don't allow yourself or anyone else to bridge them. Consider an example: Let's assume you've realized you do not like to take phone calls after 9:00 p.m. Most people set the zone at 10:00, but you have noticed that by around 8:55 your eyes start to flicker with sleep and you are ready for your cozy, comfortable bed?

Let your friends and family know that phone calls after 9:00 p.m. will not be entertained. Anyone who bridges the boundary will not receive a pickup to their call.

See how you have simplified your life? You know that phone lines and devices will go peaceably silent by 9:00 p.m. You can choose to crawl into bed or treat yourself to a nice cup of hot chocolate before doing so, all within the quiet, simple comfort of your Dot Life boundaries.

AUTOMATION HAS TAKEN OVER THE WORLD

The world is becoming more and more technology driven. This is a perfect era in which to implement a Dot Life because technology is able to support our lives in so many different ways today.

Whether you are into social media or apps or gadgets for the home such as Alexa and Echo, taking advantage of these new developments for making life easier will be a boost to your Dot Life strategy. Consider an app that may provide you with support in enhancing your home security, for instance, or an Alexa that finds recipes for your favorite chocolate cake. Let the gadgets work for you to further simplify your life.

MIND YOUR OWN BUSINESS

I don't know if I can stress this point enough: While it's worthy to be concerned about your neighbors and wish them well, or even to get into their business from time to time, it's also true that the time spent minding other people's business means less time spent in minding your own.

At the end of the day, the prep school that your neighbors want to send their kids to or the latest Mercedes that they bought (and how on Earth they were able to afford?) is really no one's business but their own.

Simplify your life by getting focused on the things that are important to moving it forward. Let others figure out their own dilemmas, especially if they did not invite you to add your two cents of advice.

CHOOSING YOUR ENVIRONMENT

I want to end this section with this topic because I believe it crowns what I've recommended for the Dot Life simplification process: Your environment is instrumental in determining how easy your life can feel or become.

As an example—without wanting to disparage any particular taste in music—would you say that a café where soft jazz is being played would feel more relaxed than one that is playing hard rock?

I would say soft jazz would win the relaxation competition, at least for most folks. In the same vein, the quality of your environment—including the type of furniture you choose, how it's arranged, scents and aromas—contributes to relaxation. As part of your Dot Life implementation, pay attention to your environment and how you can make it more relaxing—simply.

A PASSING THOUGHT ON THIS CHAPTER

As you engage more in positivity, simplification, and effectiveness, you will find that you are indulging less and less in your old habits. You are getting ripe for the final stage of the Dot Life, which is circle rebirth.

CHAPTER SEVEN

CIRCLE REBIRTH
YOUR NEW LIFE

When you have created the new positive circle for your life, your journey does not stop there. You need to stay consistent with this circle by focusing on things that add value to your life. This stage is known as circle rebirth because this new life of yours is like a newborn. Life is full of challenges, and to live a less chaotic life you need to learn how to overcome all the possible setbacks that come your way.

FOCUS ON LEARNING AND CREATING

Focus on learning and always creating. A wise person never stops learning. This is high time for you to learn things you have always wanted to learn but never had the time for. If you want to learn how to play the guitar, go for it. If you want to change your workplace, then attend a seminar that could help you decide what you want. Creativity induces more positivity.

Find activities that require creativity. Everything in this

world that is manufactured exists because of a creative mind. Move around and explore so that you learn new things. Engage in meaningful conversations with the people around you. Don't be reluctant to ask questions. Don't be reluctant to take risks. Don't be hard on yourself. Give yourself constructive criticism instead of harsh negative words. You need to live in a positive system at all times.

LIVE YOUR POSITIVE SYSTEM

Your positive system is your Dot Life. Your Dot Life becomes your way of life and everything in it aligns with one another. The more that areas within your dot mesh positively with each other, the less room there is for negative influences to invade your system.

There will always be challenges that you face, and it won't be possible to stay positive at all times, but you need to be sure to limit the impact that negative influences have on your life. This is why you need to stay in the present moment, and the best way to live in the present is by practicing mindfulness.

MINDFULNESS DOT LIFE TECHNIQUES

Mindfulness[1] is a type of meditation that has been practiced for centuries and has become a hot topic in recent years. There are many ways in which mindfulness can be practiced, but one of the good things about it is that it can be done anywhere at any time.

The simplest mindfulness technique is to take a deep

breath. This is enough to bring you back to the present moment because we forget to breathe when we are under a lot of stress.

This will also bring you back to your focus. Here is a simple mindfulness exercise that you can do anywhere at any time:

- Sit in a relaxed posture but make sure your back is straight.
- Close your eyes and focus on the sensations that you are feeling while sitting.
- Take deep long breaths. Breathe normally but deeply.
- Inhale through your nose and exhale from your mouth. Let your breathing form a rhythm. As you do that, focus on the breath moving through your body.
- Ask yourself about your intention for your day and then set up the intention. For example, "My intention for today is to focus more on positive things. I will take action to become closer to my goal."
- Pause and check yourself and your intention throughout the day.

SHARE AND GROW YOUR SYSTEM

Share your system with other people because they might be struggling with a chaotic life as well. Whenever you have the opportunity, take time to learn new things. Keep adding positive and subtracting negative things from your system.

Take some time out and reflect on your progress. Your system will grow with time. Make sure that you surround yourself with people and things that add value to your life.

Follow the format laid out in this book to achieve circle rebirth in your Home, Relationships, Business, and Social life.

HOME

It is time to restructure your home life to suit you and your lifestyle. If your goal is to entertain family and friends, spend time with your partner, or raise your kids, determine the amount of time you spend at home, the space you need, and the new, fresh things you can bring to your home now that the clutter has been cleared out during the phases of circle of control and Dot Life.

As you start with a fresh palate, consider the common areas first. Is there a room with furniture that is seldom used? Determine how to repurpose that room.

If you host multiple functions at home per year, evaluate your space and remove unnecessary knick-knacks.

Consider simple decorations that are inviting and make your space look fresh and enjoyable.

If you are the entertaining type who likes to cook, let your space reflect your passion for the kitchen. Perhaps have a few decorations around the living room area that suggest your love of entertaining.

These are only some of the things that you could

implement in your home life to perfect the restructure that your circle rebirth has now begun. I want to expound on these tips, so let me suggest a few additional things you could add to make your home viable for circle rebirth.

NATURE IN THE HOME

Plants and flowers are parts of nature that contribute to a relaxing, beautiful environment. Their ability to calm and beautify a home cannot be over-emphasized. Even if you are a man who doesn't think of flowers as a therapeutic option for males, or a woman who doesn't think she should be allowed near plants because she doesn't have a green thumb, the presence of these natural elements in the home are an excellent addition to the completion of a circle rebirth for a simplified, Zen place to live.

If you are truly concerned that plants may die under your care, there is a wide variety of options for artificial greenery available for interior and exterior use today. Visit your local home design stores, including popular places like Ikea, and you will find beautiful plant options that would add to the aesthetic of your home and convert it into a glorious, relaxing environment that demonstrates your rebirth into that perfect life circle of ease.

COLORS ARE YOUR FRIENDS

Although some people prefer a palette of dark and moody shades in their home, I would suggest that a circle rebirth is more readily demonstrated with shades that are light and airy.

Light, bright colors and airiness (rather than clunky, stuffy decor and cluttered space) are evidence of a home that has been cleared of unnecessary junk and of someone who has embraced the minimalist nature of a Dot Life.

Decorate your haven—otherwise known as your home space—with brightly colored cushions, throws, and even rugs. Surprise the visitor entering your place and let them be dazzled by the welcoming lightness of furniture and meaningful use of space.

THINGS THAT SAY "THIS IS MY PLACE"

A circle rebirth is going to give you a new signature—think of it as a new brand. Your life will be decluttered to the extent that you now have room to reinvent yourself and your home. You will start selecting home pieces that represent new tastes and preferences that perhaps you have dreamt about but could never implement because of the chaotic surroundings in which you previously lived.

Now is the time to show off your unique tastes. Surround yourself with art, textures, furniture pieces, or any other unique, identifying marks that will boldly say: This is my circle rebirth, and I am living it to the fullest!

A READING NOOK

Studying and reading are a couple of the activities that help us to develop into improved people. We study to learn new ideas, and when we read, we gain fresh knowledge and perspectives about the world around us.

Consider including a tribute to education and self-improvement in your home as part of your circle rebirth. Implement a reading nook into your home. Have a corner where you can retreat to read, study, or meditate on new things that you have learned. Make it cozy and comfortable. Perhaps lay a snug rug in the corner, add an armchair, and grace it with a bookshelf filled with your favorite books and reading material. You will be proud of your little space as another testament to the circle rebirth that has happened to you!

Your home is not the only area that will show your new circle rebirth. You want to consider other parts of your life as well, such as your relationships and business. I will speak to each of these.

RELATIONSHIPS

I see a lot of relationships that focus on others. Although there are times when we must focus our dots on care for our kids, family, friends, and associates, we must not allow ourselves to become overwhelmed in the process.

The key to balancing these relationships depends on the specifics of each, and how you are able to effectively contribute to a desirable outcome for them as well as for yourself. Every situation is different and every situation has its own challenges. Having a focused approach will make it easier.

There are some particularly wise choices that you can

make in relationships that will enhance the quality of your circle rebirth, and we will discuss these next.

BUILDING TRUST IN YOUR RELATIONSHIPS

There is no doubt that a trustful relationship breeds ease and will tend to be an enjoyable one. Such relationships are one essential in a life of circle rebirth. Relationships are necessary in all of our lives and the more peaceful they are, the simpler our lives will be.

Having reached this section of the book and having navigated through understanding the reasons behind a chaotic life and understanding the concepts of the perfect Dot Life, your circle rebirth will now take you on a journey into your relationships to ensure that the other people in your life experience rebirth as well. This rebirth begins with building trust. Your circle rebirth will enhance the way you treat people, an improvement that you will notice in yourself too; the people you interact with will be aware of your character of dependability.

I will expound upon the principles of organizing a chaotic life to a deeper extent in another book but having been introduced to those principles in *this* book, your more organized sense of life and self will help you remarkably in meeting any promises that you express to others.

For example, if you promise your son or your spouse that you will meet them for dinner at 6:00 p.m., and you used to be a person who had time-management issues, your new Dot Life will enable you to manage your time effectively so you keep your promises. As the people in your life start to notice that you set a time and you keep it, their trust in you increases.

This is only one simple example, but it can be repeated in many areas of your life.

MINDFULNESS IS YOUR FRIEND

You may have many friends but be sure that mindfulness is one of them. It is defined as a state of being aware. As you begin to understand your circle rebirth, it is essential that you increase your level of awareness of the people and circumstances around you.

A mindful person is not ruled by their emotions, but they are constantly cognizant of their environment, including the emotions of the people around them. They tailor their words and their actions to suit the situations and the different personalities they interact with so that—in every circumstance—they experience the ultimate results for their expectations.

A circle rebirth means that you want to start experiencing life in this way.

TIME TO TOLERATE OTHER VIEWS DIFFERENT FROM YOURS

A circle rebirth means that your tolerance threshold has increased. As an example, let us say in the past, knowing that you are an expert in one field or another, you discount the opinions of laymen or people who are not as well versed in the field as you. But as a person who is now practicing circle rebirth, your mindset should change.

Let us say that you are an expert fisherman. You know your bait, you have excellent knowledge of fishing rods, and for goodness' sake, no one has a better technique for reeling in those aquatic creatures than you do! You happen to meet a newbie who just got started fishing about a year ago and thinks he has the "in" knowledge about how to fish.

As a person who is tolerant of others' views, you will listen to their opinions about what they've learned so far about fishing, what they think has worked best for them, and so on. You may even buy in to some of their newbie knowledge and try it out yourself sometime.

The key is to be able to accept their views and eagerness on the subject without the sense that you are so advanced that you cannot listen to them or take them seriously. A person who has a circle rebirth has become a tolerant person who accepts diverse views. In the example of these fishermen, the newbie's views about techniques, best equipment, and more may not be the same as yours, but this is a chance to demonstrate circle rebirth by not shutting them down, and instead, accepting them.

SHOWING APPRECIATION

It is a sad fact that our world has become so chaotic and unmindful that simple practices such as appreciating other people are no longer common.

Whatever happened to saying "thank you" when someone holds a door open for the next person coming into a room? Or leaving a note on the refrigerator for a spouse to acknowledge that you really appreciate how they went to the trouble of making dinner the previous night?

Appreciation is one of the keys to building strong, lasting relationships. The people who we appreciate will remember it. As the saying goes, people will forget what you said and what you did, but they will never forget how you made them feel.

Therefore, appreciate your people as a part of practicing circle rebirth. Let them carry that forever feeling of having known or met someone who held them in honor.

THE OTHER AREA TO FOCUS UPON

In addition to your relationships, another area that requires attention during a circle rebirth is your business or career. Since this is the place where you earn your living, it needs ample attention so that you are able to convert it into a rebirthed circle too.

Business or Career

At this phase of your life's decluttering process, your career or business should have a clear focus and align with your goals and passions.

You are now able to set and reach targets without self-inflicted obstacles and are prepared to manage unforeseen business issues that arise.

Positioning yourself with control and options leads to more success and less fear of taking risks. Your previous dependency on factors involving poor credit, antiquated systems, debt, and poor planning are no longer distractions keeping you from moving forward on your life's objectives.

Once you have established some dependable business or career goals and have eliminated negative factors, you are now ripe for creating "wealth for happiness." At this point, creating residual investment or financial planning goals are the center of your dot.

These goals must align with your objectives for the life you want to live. We are not simply looking to obtain wealth to achieve the status or goal of "being wealthy." There are miserable people who exist at all levels of the income spectrum. Working seven days a week to achieve a financial goal doesn't make sense if you can't meet the important factors within your dot along the way. There must be a balance. Aligning your business or job goals with your passions will complete the Dot Life you aspire to and enjoy.

Waking up and looking forward to how I can create something that will improve or benefit others is the best feeling in the world to me. You might be wondering what are some ways that *you* can experience a circle rebirth in your business?

I can think of a few to discuss in this section.

TAKE CARE OF YOURSELF

This should be the absolute first rule in your circle rebirth for your business. In today's world, life is extremely hectic. One may find themselves eating TV dinners often or grabbing junk food on the go because of insufficient time to plan or prepare a healthy meal. Exercise and taking care of fitness is often placed on the back burner in the racing world of career and professions.

In a circle rebirth, it is essential to press the "slow down" or "stop" button.

Take a breather, pause for a moment to relax. The work will always be there, even if it has a deadline. Your health is another story; if you don't pay enough attention to it, it may not always be there.

Thus, pause and take care of yourself as part of a successful circle rebirth.

MAKE PLANNING A NECESSITY

Making plans to get things done is also instrumental in achieving self-care and a host of other things that are needed for a full circle rebirth life.

Plan your meals. Plan your work outs. Plan your day. Even if things do not go according to schedule, your day will be more organized than one where you're operating according to a "fly by the seat of the pants" schedule.

GREAT SERVICE MAKES A BUSINESS GREAT

In a circle rebirth, one of the brands in your place of business must be "good service." It does not matter what type of work you do or how well you are getting paid—assuming you work for someone else. An attitude of "I will give it my best" is going to be the attitude that takes you to the next stage of success.

That is the mindset that a person who is operating in a perfect circle will adopt. Imagine the reduction in customer service calls or office visits with the manager. Think of the host of problems that could be avoided if the service was great the first time. It is the key to a peaceful business life, and after all, peace is what you are trying to achieve in your circle rebirth.

THE ART OF MONEY MANAGEMENT

It is important not to underestimate how good money management can be the key to a peaceful business and career. If we are able to manage the funds from our job or business well, there is a lot to be gained. That will flow into other sections of our life, providing funds to take care of our family's daily needs and to do the things we enjoy.

Thus, money management should be at the forefront of a business whose owner is practicing circle rebirth. Manage your money well and you will manage your circle rebirth well.

AFTERWORD

Life is full of surprises and challenges. For me, the challenges are far easier to manage when I am tackling them without trying to manage chaos in the process. Eliminating distractions has allowed me to take on challenges with focus and to resolve not to disturb my Dot Life lifestyle. With chaos in the mix, I allowed vices and negative influences to rear their ugly heads in the narrative my life had become. I would take a break from the problems and issues that I faced only to watch them compound into bigger problems in the future. Learning to disassociate myself from anything negative that was not providing me with positive energy took time, however, it has become an instilled focus and way of life for me.

We do certain things in a certain way each day, and they become a part of our routine. The actions we repeat in our everyday life become our habits, and habits can be both good and bad. We need to realize what our bad habits are.

After that realization, we need to actively take steps

that can help us eliminate those habits. It might seem like —no matter what we do—we always fall back on our bad habits. That is what happens when we are not mentally prepared to accept a change in our lives. We need to prepare mentally for the new substantial changes in our lives.

Transforming a chaotic life into a more ordered life is a journey. It does not happen overnight, and it has various stages. You need to pass through all the stages on your way to achieving an ordered life.

Setbacks are a part of life, and you need to remain steadfast during hard times. Become aware of your behavior and you should remain consistent. It is never too late to develop a change in your life; all you need to do is take action instantly!

`

NOTES

INTRODUCTION

1. Gogh, Vincent van. "Self-Portrait." The Art Institute of Chicago. Painting and Sculpture of Europe, January 1, 1887. https://www.artic.edu/artworks/80607/self-portrait.

1. MY DOT STORY

1. Singh, Manoj. "The 2007–2008 Financial Crisis in Review." Investopedia, March 26, 2023. https://www.investopedia.com/articles/economics/09/financial-crisis-review.asp.

2. CIRCLE OF LIFE

1. "Chaos Theory." Encyclopædia Britannica. Encyclopædia Britannica, inc., February 19, 2023. https://www.britannica.com/science/chaos-theory.

5. CIRCLE OF CONTROL

1. "Everything You Need to Know about Smart Goals." AchieveIt, November 11, 2022. https://www.achieveit.com/resources/blog/everything-you-need-to-know-about-smart-goals/.

6. DOT LIFE

1. "Minimalism Definition & Meaning." Merriam-Webster. Merriam-Webster. Accessed March 31, 2023. https://www.merriam-webster.com/dictionary/minimalism.
2. Singh, Rachna. "What Can Buddhism and Minimalism Teach Us." Now with Purpose, January 28, 2023. https://nowwithpurpose.-

com/buddhism-and-minimalism/.

7. CIRCLE REBIRTH

1. Cherry, Kendra. "Learn How to Make a Mindfulness Meditation Practice Part of Your Day." Verywell Mind. Verywell Mind, September 22, 2022. https://www.verywellmind.com/mindfulness-meditation-88369.

ACKNOWLEDGMENTS

To My Mentor:

Michael Tompkins, you may not realize it, however, I want to acknowledge my sincere gratitude for your quiet leadership examples in life and business. The examples rang loud, my friend.